GW00786490

The Essential

Guide to
WHALES

Mike Bruton

DAVID PHILIP PUBLISHERS
Cape Town

in association with

THE MTN CAPE WHALE ROUTE
Cape Town

First published 1998 in southern Africa by David Philip
Publishers (Pty) Ltd, 208 Werdmuller Centre, Claremont
7708, South Africa; in association with the MTN Cape
Whale Route, P O Box 797, Howard Place, Cape Town,
8000

ISBN 0-86486-348-9

The MTN Cape Whale Route stretches along 900 km of
the Cape Coast from Doringbaai on the West Coast to the
Tsitsikamma National Park on the East Coast. It promotes
eco-tourism and marine conservation both locally and
internationally and focuses on marine mammal education.

ERRATA: Essential Guide to Whales

* On page 39 the heading in the left-hand column
should read **Bryde's whale**, and that in the right-
hand column should read **Southern right whale**.

* On the inside of the dustjacket, the cover
photograph should be identified as a **humpback
whale**.

Printed in South Africa by ABC Press (Pty) Ltd, 21
Kinghall Avenue, Epping, South Africa

CONTENTS

3

4 *Whaling in Table Bay in the nineteenth century.*

PREFACE

Watching whales is the ultimate wildlife experience. Who can resist the thrill of a 50-ton southern right whale launching itself into the air and crashing down with a gigantic splash, or the spectacle of a school of dolphins playfully surfing in the waves? While dolphins have always been visible off our coast, the whales disappeared for many years as a result of whaling, and they are only now returning. We are the privileged generation who can, for the first time in many years, glimpse their hidden lives beneath and above the waves. The results of one of the most successful marine conservation programmes ever undertaken are unfolding before our eyes.

Many people thought that the whales were doomed when their populations were reduced to extremely low levels by commercial whaling in the eighteenth and nineteenth centuries. Some whale populations may never recover, and many will remain only as remnants of their former magnificence. However, the southern right whale off the South African coast is showing a recovery that almost defies belief. From a post-whaling population of just a few hundred individuals 40 years ago, they have increased to over 2 000 animals now, which is still only 10% of the original population size. They are, however, increasing at a phenomenal rate of 7–8% each year, one of the highest rates of increase in the world, which means that the population size will double every ten years.

The joy to us as land animals is that, as the whale numbers increase, they become more and more visible around our coast. We can all participate in the celebration of the return of the southern right whales from the brink of extinction.

It is important to realise, though, that there is not just one species of whale in our seas, but several species. Some are no longer in danger of extinction, whereas others are still threatened. Some are large, others small, but they are all beautifully adapted to the marine environment. We can all play a role in whale and dolphin conservation by knowing them better and ensuring that our own direct and indirect actions do not impact negatively on them and on their environment. This book is a first step in that direction.

Happy whale watching.

Mike Bruton
Cape Town
May 1998

Introduction to whales

The relationship between whales and people in South Africa has passed through three distinct phases. For over 1800 years the Khoi-San people used the meat, blubber and oil of whales washed up on the beach as a source of food. This opportunistic use of whale products made no impact on whale populations and was sustainable in the long term.

With the advent of whaling in South Africa in 1785, southern right whales, blue whales and humpback whales were extensively and unsustainably harvested, mainly for the benefit of foreign whalers. This second phase was short but devastating and whale numbers declined dramatically. Worldwide, the stocks of blue whales and humpback whales were reduced to 6 and 7% of their original numbers. After whales were first formally protected in 1935, their numbers started to recover and they began to be appreciated again as an important component of South Africa's marine life.

The burgeoning conservation movement and the initiation of whale research brought about a new relationship with whales based on respect and harmony. Whales became the icon of the conservation movement and many people identified with efforts to bring them back from the brink of extinction. Whale watching is now one of the most compelling tourist attractions worldwide and forms the basis of a growing tourism industry that is changing people's relationship with the sea. This third phase will hopefully be sustainable in the long term, although there is some debate about the potential impact of boat-based whale watching.

The origin of whales

Animals first evolved in the sea at a time when the land was too hot and dry to support life. The dominant vertebrates or backboned group of animals then (and now) were the fishes. From the fishes the four-legged animals or tetrapods evolved – the amphibians, reptiles, birds and mammals. The amphibians have always been a small but ecologically important group, linking freshwater and terrestrial habitats. The reptiles were for a long time the dominant animal group on land – the spectacular dinosaurs or terrible lizards produced species that were the largest animals ever to live on land. What is less well known is that the reptiles evolved forms that also dominated the skies and waters of the planet for many millions of years.

About 250 million years ago some of the reptiles in the seas evolved into species that resembled our modern-day dolphins and small whales. Today the only large marine reptiles are the sea turtles, which inhabit all the warm oceans of the world, and the Komodo dragons and their relatives from Pacific Ocean islands.

No-one knows for sure what caused the dinosaurs to become extinct, but they did not disappear completely, as the modern crocodiles are directly descended from one branch of them, as is the interesting little tuatara, a lizard that lives on islands near New Zealand. The most popular explanation is that a large meteorite hit the planet and caused major climatic disruptions which destroyed the food resources necessary to support large land animals.

The mammals first evolved during the dinosaur era. Initially they were small and largely nocturnal, as they provided little competition for their giant, voracious competitors. After the extinction of the dinosaurs about 65 million years ago, the mammals were able to gain a competitive advantage, but not before the birds had made a strong bid to be the dominant vertebrate group on land. At one stage in evolution giant flightless birds, with heads the size of a horse's head, roamed the land and provided stiff competition for the mammals. The dominance of the birds on land did not last, however, possibly because their egg-laying method of breeding was less efficient than the live-bearing mode of the mammals.

The success of the mammals later extended into the sea. Palaeontological, genetic and biochemical evidence suggests that about 55 million years ago a four-legged terrestrial animal that resembled a wolf with hooves (called *Mesonyx*) moved into, and became progressively better adapted to living in, the sea. The earliest whales or archaeocetes lived between 38 and 55 million years ago. They probably evolved to fill the niche left vacant by the extinction of the giant reptiles about 65 million years ago. Fossils of the earliest archaeocetes indicate that they had hind limbs and small heads. A later group, which lived between

9

38 and 43 million years ago (called the zeuglodons), had lost their hind limbs but still had a vestigial pelvis and femur. About 38 million years ago the archaeocetes largely disappeared from the fossil record.

About 30 to 40 million years ago the two groups of modern whales, the odontocetes (now the toothed whales, dolphins and porpoises) and the mysticetes (baleen whales) evolved rapidly. These groups are jointly termed the cetaceans. Today about 80 species of cetaceans are found around the world. Surprisingly not all species live in the sea; four dolphin species live in freshwater, one each in the Amazon (and Orinoco), Ganges, Indus and Yangtse River systems. Marine cetaceans are found in all the world's oceans from the Arctic to the Antarctic.

During their evolution whales, dolphins and porpoises have undergone a number of adaptations for life in seas and rivers. The most important adaptation is the loss of the pelvis and hind limbs. All that remain of these bones and limbs today are vestigial pelvic bones. Other adaptations to the aquatic environment are the streamlining of the body and the almost total loss of hair. Cetacean ears now comprise tiny ear holes situated between the eyes.

Whales and dolphins have retained the mammalian method of breeding, even though they live under the water. The young are born in the sea and resemble miniature adults. The mother suckles the young and feeds them a very rich milk. The one reproductive innovation is that the male organs are contained inside the body, probably for streamlining.

The nostrils of cetaceans have moved to the top of the head to form the blow hole. All baleen whales have a double blow hole, while the toothed whales, dolphins and porpoises have a single blow hole.

The fore limbs of modern whales and dolphins have evolved into flippers that are flattened and blade-like and are used for stability and steering. The tail has horizontal flukes which, combined with the modified spine and back muscles, have evolved to provide propulsion. It is the upstroke of the tail that generates the forward movement in dolphins and whales.

The fact that they no longer have to support their body weight on their limbs has allowed some whales to become very large. The largest of the whales, the blue whale, is the largest mammal that has ever lived. They have been recorded at over 33 metres in length and 190 tons in weight, although the average size is much smaller at 25 m for males and 26 m for females.

What is a mammal?

Mammals are a group of advanced, four-legged backboned animals that usually have fur, suckle their young and breathe air. Along with the birds, the mammals are warm-blooded and so can remain active at night and in cold environments. Their covering of hair and a layer of fat beneath the skin also help to conserve body heat. Mammals first evolved on land from the reptiles about 200 million years ago. They remained relatively small and inconspicuous until the dinosaurs died out, when they evolved rapidly and became the dominant backboned animals on land. Mammals differ from reptiles in the positions of their limbs which are held more vertically beneath the body. This allows them to run more efficiently. Furthermore, their teeth have evolved into a number of different types as an adaptation to different diets. Mammals have relatively large brains and are capable of complex and adaptive behaviour.

The mammals are divided into three major groups, the monotremes (egg-laying mammals represented only by the platypus and the echidna), marsupials (kangaroos, wallabies, and their kin) and the placentals (all the other more familiar mammals, including monkeys, giraffes, antelopes, lions, bears, horses, rats, bats, whales and man). There are about 4 000 species of living mammals worldwide, of which nearly half are rodents (rats and mice) and about a quarter are bats.

The cetaceans (whales, dolphins and porpoises) are one of several groups of mammals that have returned to the sea from land. Other mammals that now live in the sea include seals, sea lions, elephant seals, dugongs, manatees and sea otters.

What is a whale?

Whales, dolphins and porpoises all belong to the group of aquatic mammals called the cetaceans. The cetaceans can be divided into the baleen whales and the toothed whales, dolphins and porpoises. They range in size from about one metre long in some dolphins to over 33 metres in the blue whale. The term 'whale' refers to any cetacean over 3–4 m long and applies to both groups, as the killer whales and the pilot whales are actually large dolphins. Porpoises are a family of small dolphins and none are found off the South African coast.

At first glance many small whales and dolphins look like fishes, especially sharks. The whale shark, in particular, with its enormous body and huge tail fin, resembles a fin whale. But whales are mammals, and are more closely related to people and other mammals than they are to fishes. A useful way to distinguish a whale from a fish is in the shape of the tail: a whale's tail is horizontal and moves up and down, whereas a fish's tail is (typically) vertical and moves from side to side. Furthermore, fishes do not need to rise to the surface to breathe (although there are exceptions) as they use their gills to extract oxygen from the water. Whales have to rise to the surface to breathe, and they expel the used air through their blow holes.

Most fishes have a covering of scales or scutes on their bodies, whereas whales have a smooth skin. Most fishes lay large numbers of small eggs which are abandoned after fertilisation, although a few guard their eggs and young or are live-bearers. All whales are live-bearers and they usually produce one young at a time. The young are protected for many months by the mother and sometimes by an assistant whale.

Anatomy of a whale

Because they no longer have to use their limbs to support their weight on land, whales tend to be large animals with bulky bodies. Early whales had small heads but modern whales have enormous heads that may be up to one third the length of the body. They typically have cavernous mouths.

Whales are supremely adapted to underwater life. They have streamlined bodies and have lost most of their body hair, probably to improve streamlining, although some very young calves have hair. The thick coats of hair possessed by other mammals have been replaced by a layer of insulating fat known as blubber, which helps to keep the whale warm. The blubber, which also acts as a food source, can be up to 50 centimetres thick in some species. Some researchers have found that whales may have a problem keeping cool, rather than keeping warm. They are therefore able to pump blood into their flippers and flukes, which are richly endowed with surface blood vessels, in order to transfer body heat into the water or air.

Whales have short, stiff necks which enable them to swim strongly and at high speed. Their front limbs have turned into powerful flippers and their hind limbs have disappeared. They have huge muscular tails which are their main means of propulsion. Their nostrils have moved to the top of the head so that they can easily take a breath and expel used air at the water surface.

Whales, like other mammals, have five major senses – sight, smell, hearing, taste and touch. They have developed strong eye muscles that can change the shape of the eye lens for both above- and underwater vision. The eyes of many whales are near the back of the head, which means that they have monocular vision, i.e. the arcs of vision of the two eyes do not overlap. They have to turn their head to one side in order to see forwards.

The skin of a whale is highly sensitive to touch and is able to detect subtle changes in water pressure as well as the bow waves of other whales. The senses of taste and smell have probably been almost lost in whales and dolphins. Whales are probably able to detect the magnetic field of the Earth through a magnetic sense that they use during migrations.

Conversely, the hearing sense of whales and dolphins is acute. Some whales communicate over great distances (probably hundreds of kilometres), as sound carries very well under water. Toothed whales and dolphins are able to determine their distance from other objects using echolocation. They emit clicks and interpret their relative position based on the time taken for the clicks to be returned. Dolphins are known to be able to tell the size, shape, position, surface characteristics and movements of an object using echolocation.

Whales are capable of making a wide variety of sounds underwater. The best-known vocalisations are the songs of the humpback whales, which sing structured songs on their breeding-grounds. All the males on the breeding ground sing the same song in order to compete for females. Toothed whales make two kinds of sounds, pulsed clicks, which are used in echolocation, and unpulsed whistles, squawks, groans and moans, which may have a social function. Baleen whales make very different sounds, generally of a lower frequency and longer duration. The moans are probably used to locate large targets such as shoals of prey. Humpback whales sing long (20 minutes or more) songs that are transmitted over vast distances in the ocean and probably serve to maintain social contact.

The whale has the largest brain of any mammal, and the largest brain of any animal that has ever existed. Brain size is, however, not an adequate measure of intelligence on its own. Whales have very small brains in relation to their body size. They do unquestionably show intelligent behaviour, especially when they behave in groups and communicate with one another using complex songs. Studies of small whales and dolphins in captivity have revealed that they are readily trained to perform complex acts and can also solve simple problems, although they do not score more highly than some terrestrial mammals.

Whales, unlike man, are well adapted for deep diving without ill-effects as they have a high tolerance of carbon dioxide and are two or three times more efficient than land animals at extracting oxygen from inhaled air. Furthermore, the rib cages of whales are able to collapse during deep dives and they have layers of insulating fat to keep them warm in very cold water. Whereas humans experience the bends, caused by the release of nitrogen bubbles into the blood, if they do not decompress properly after a deep dive, whales do not have to decompress at all. Sperm whales have been recorded to ascend from a dive at the astounding rate of 90 to 150 metres per minute! In whales the diaphragm is set at an oblique angle and almost all the air is squeezed out of the lungs during a dive. As a result, no nitrogen can be absorbed by the blood. In cetaceans and seals, the lungs are able to collapse completely under pressure without damage, whereas in man a collapse of the lungs causes blood capillaries to rupture. Whales are also able to lower their metabolic rate during a dive so as to reduce their oxygen consumption.

The two groups of whales

The main differences between the two groups of cetaceans, the baleen whales and the toothed whales, are in their feeding apparatus and habits. Baleen whales have large plates of baleen hanging from their upper jaws. These baleen plates are made from keratin (similar to our fingernails) and may be up to three metres long in the bowhead whale. The inner edge of the baleen is fringed with a dense mat of loose hairs that sieve the prey from the water. There are eight species of baleen whales in South African waters. Toothed whales and dolphins have teeth to capture and chew their prey (mainly fish and squid). The beaked whales have few teeth, and

17

Skeleton of a baleen whale showing the huge jaw bones from which the baleen hangs. (Photo: Mike Bruton)

their method of catching prey has not as yet been discovered. Twenty-nine species of toothed whales have been recorded off South Africa.

The great whales comprise the baleen whales and the sperm whale (which is toothed). The baleen whales include the rorqual whales (whales with pleated throats that balloon during feeding – the blue, sei, fin, minke, Bryde's and humpback whales), the right whales (northern, southern and pygmy right whales and the bowhead whale), and the gray whale.

The least known of all the whales are the beaked whales, which inhabit deep open ocean waters. One species, the lesser beaked whale, was only discovered in 1976, while a further species, Longman's beaked whale, has never been seen alive in the wild and is only known from two skulls found on beaches. A high diversity of beaked whales (eight species) has been recorded off the South African coast, but they are poorly known.

Almost all of the baleen whales undertake seasonal migrations each year from breeding-grounds in warm waters to feeding-grounds in cold polar waters. Bryde's whale remains in warm waters throughout the year.

Whale migrations are a compromise between the feeding and breeding requirements of the animals. Baleen whales are filter feeders and require dense concentrations of their prey that are found only in cold, high latitude oceans. However, new-born whale calves may not be able to tolerate the very cold waters, and consequently calving must

19

occur in warmer waters. Little or no feeding occurs during the breeding migration; during this time the animal relies on the blubber reserve that it has laid down during the feeding season.

Whales in South Africa

There are about 80 species of whales, dolphins and porpoises (cetaceans) worldwide, but more are likely to be discovered. Thirty-seven species occur off southern Africa (46% of the world total), which is a high diversity compared to the 25 species in the north Atlantic Ocean and 28 species in the north Pacific Ocean. The relatively large number of whale and dolphin species off our coast is due to the high diversity of habitats caused by the meeting off our shores of the cold Atlantic Ocean and the warm Indian Ocean. The upwelling on the west coast that brings food-rich water to the surface also attracts whales and dolphins. Furthermore, South Africa is close to the Antarctic where the great baleen whales go to feed on krill, and has a number of wide, shallow bays along its south coast that are suitable habitats for breeding by baleen whales.

The most commonly seen whale off the South African coast is the **southern right whale** *Eubalaena australis*. It was given this name because it was the 'right' whale for early whalers to catch as it was slow enough to be caught by open-boat whalers, inhabited inshore areas, floated after being harpooned and produced high yields of oil, meat and baleen ('whale bone'). Most other whales sink after being harpooned and are difficult to recover. The scientific name is derived from *eu* (Greek for right), *balaena* (Latin for whale) and *australis* (Latin for southern). They are found off the coasts of South America, Africa, Australia and New Zealand between latitudes 20° S and 55° S, rarely 65° S.

Right whales are characterised by the presence of white callosities on their heads, the distinct notch in the centre of the sharply pointed tail flukes, the broad back with no dorsal fin, the strongly arched mouthline and the absence of throat grooves. They are usually black to blue-black on the upper body and paler below. The southern right whale produces a V-shaped blow of water vapour (which may be up to 5 metres high) from its blow hole whereas the blow of all other whales is in a single column. Furthermore, every other baleen whale has a dorsal fin. Adult southern right whales range in length between 12.5 and 15.5 metres (rarely 18 metres) with an average length of about 13.9 metres (the length of 10 elephants) and a weight of 29 to 58 tons (average 41 tons). The calves weigh about one ton at birth and measure 4.5 to 6 metres in length.

The callosities on the heads of whales have no known function except that the males may use them to scratch other males when they are fighting. The callosities are inhabited by whale lice, small parasitic crustaceans that crawl around on their skin, and by barnacles. The lice and barnacles spend their entire lives on the whale and are not true parasites as they do not harm the whale. The lice do

Callosities on the head of a southern right whale.
(Photo: Ken Findlay)

seem to irritate the whales, which attempt to scratch them off by rubbing their heads against kelp. The lice make the callosities appear pink, yellow or orange. Each whale has a different pattern of callosities, which makes them very easy to tell apart. The large callosity that is often found at the tip of the snout of these whales is called the 'bonnet' in whaler's parlance.

The whale lice feed on the dead, outer layers of the whale's skin, whereas the barnacles filter-feed from the water column itself. The barnacles are embedded 3–4 cm into the skin of the whales and first settle onto the whales when they are calves in shallow water. Even young calves less than one month old have callosity patterns on their heads.

Southern right whales normally swim at speeds of 0.5 to 4 kilometres per hour but may reach top speeds of 17 kilometres per hour. They dive to a maximum depth of over 300 metres and can hold their breath for over 30 minutes. Their life span is unknown but is thought to exceed 50 years. The baleen plates on this species form a giant sieve and are 2 metres long and 30 cm wide, hanging down from the roof of the mouth.

Southern right whales were widespread in the southern hemisphere until the late 1700s, probably numbering over 20 000 animals. At this time they occurred in southern Africa off the coasts of South Africa, Namibia and Mozambique. They were very abundant in the waters off Cape Town according to the accounts of Jan van Riebeeck and other early visitors to the Cape. By 1775 whaling vessels from America were overwintering at the Cape and in 1792 the first southern right whales were taken from shore-based boats by Cape colonists in Table Bay.

Southern right whales were almost exterminated by open-boat whalers between 1785 and 1805 when about 12 000 whales were killed along the southern African coastline between Walvis (whale) Bay and Delagoa Bay (now Maputo Bay). Nearly all these whales were taken by American, British and French vessels and at the peak of the fishery there may have been as many as 65 whaling vessels operating off the South African coast at the same time. Each whaler would carry three or four whaleboats which were launched at first light in the morning and rowed or sailed around the coastal bays in search of prey.

The principal targets of the whalers were mothers with their young calves and it is not surprising therefore that the population collapsed and the catches declined. Whaling efforts still continued for many years, however, as whale products fetched a handsome profit, and whales were relatively cheap to catch. The shore-based whale fishery continued unabated throughout the 19th and into the early 20th century. Whaling stations were established at various times at St Helena Bay and Table Bay on the west coast, False Bay, Betty's Bay, Plettenberg Bay and Algoa Bay on the south coast and Durban on the east coast. The last recorded southern right whale to be taken from an open boat with a hand harpoon in South African waters was in False Bay in

1929. South Africans killed about 1580 whales from open boats, a small fraction of the total taken by whalers of all nations.

Modern whaling, using steam-powered steel-hulled catchers with a harpoon cannon mounted in the bows, began in South African waters in 1908, and by 1938 a further 84 right whales had been killed from land stations at Durban, Saldanha Bay, Hangklip, Mossel Bay and Plettenberg Bay. The low catch rate (an average of less than three each year), despite the advanced catching technology and a high demand for whale products, indicates that the right whale population had reached an extremely low level after 150 years of exploitation.

Their numbers were so severely depleted that they are now rarely seen off Namibia and Mozambique. Today they frequent the western, northern and eastern Cape coasts of South Africa between June and December (usually July–November) when they visit our warm, shallow waters for calving and mating.

Southern right whales were the first of the large whales to be protected from exploitation (in 1935). In 1995 their population off southern Africa totalled about 2 000 animals out of a world population of about 5 000. They are currently increasing at a rate of 7–8% a year, which means that their population will double about every 10 years. This is one of the highest population recovery rates of any whale species in the world and higher than the recovery rate of the same species off Australia. A rate of increase of 7–8%, which has also been recorded off Argentina, is near the maximum attainable by this species and indicates that it has a high survival rate and a high breeding rate. The calving interval of right whales is known to be about 3 years in the southern hemisphere and about 4 years in the northern hemisphere.

Southern right whales mate in winter off South Africa and the gestation period is 12 months. The calves are about 6 metres long when they are born (the length of five elephants). They grow at a rate of 3 cm a day and feed on almost 600 litres of milk per day while suckling. About 4% of the calves that are born are white or albinistic but they all turn grey as adults. One well-known whale with prominent white markings, nicknamed 'Cover Girl' by whale researcher Dr Peter Best, has produced several white calves in the bay at De Hoop Nature Reserve, the most recent in 1997.

The **pygmy right whale** *Caperia marginata* is the smallest of all the baleen whales and is mostly known from widely dispersed strandings. They have a strongly arched mouth, a streamlined head and prominent dorsal fin and white baleen. They reach a weight of about 3.5 tons and are very poorly known.

The second most common whale off South Africa is the **humpback whale** *Megaptera novaeangliae*, one of the larger baleen whales. This species is recognised by its very long, narrow flippers (almost one-third of the body length), the long grooves on the throat, the serrated trailing edges to the tail flukes, the knobs on the head and lower jaw, and the small dorsal fin, which is positioned far back on the body. They have a distinctive bushy blow that is about 2.5 to 3 metres high.

Humpbacks are rorqual whales, as they have pleats or grooves on their throats. While they are filter-feeding their throats are filled with a huge volume of water and their throat muscles push the water across the baleen. Individual humpbacks are recognisable by the pattern of scarring and white patches on the undersurface of their tail fins. They can also be recognised from the white patterns on the sides of the body and from their tattered fins.

Humpbacks are amongst the most energetic of the large whales and are well known for their spectacular breaching, lobtailing and flipper-slapping behaviour. Breaches vary from a full leap clear of the water to a leisurely surge with less than half of the body emerging. Breaching may be more common at breeding-grounds and in strong winds, and usually occurs around midday.

Humpbacks reach a length of over 15 metres and have a worldwide distribution. Humpbacks are notoriously inquisitive and will often approach boats. They are slow swimmers and their dives usually last 3 to 9 minutes (sometimes up to 45 minutes). The males can be very aggressive towards one another when competing for females on the breeding-grounds.

Humpbacks are found in the northern and southern hemispheres. They feed in high-latitude, polar waters and breed in warmer waters, migrating thousands of kilometres between the two. They spend most of the year close to continental shores or islands, breeding and feeding on shallow banks, but they migrate across open seas. They feed on krill and other midwater crustaceans as well as on fishes. They have developed an incredible 'bubble-netting' method of feeding whereby they swim round in a spiral, beneath a shoal of fish or krill, blowing out air from their blow holes and enveloping their prey in a net of bubbles. They then swim with their mouths open upwards through the prey, gulping it down! They are also known to stun their prey with slaps of the flippers or flukes. Adult humpbacks weigh 25 to 30 tons, and juveniles 1 to 2 tons at birth.

More than 100 000 humpbacks were killed worldwide by whalers and, although some stocks seem to be recovering, they are a fraction of their former size. The population of humpback whales in the South Atlantic Ocean probably exceeded 30–40 000 before whaling depleted their numbers.

The most abundant and second smallest baleen whale in the world (only 10 m long), the **minke whale** *Balaenoptera acutorostrata*, also occurs off South Africa. It has a pointed snout, prominent throat grooves, a ridge on the head and pale-cream baleen plates edged with black. This species is a fast swimmer (30 km/h) that may suddenly appear next to a boat and then disappear just as quickly. They feed on krill and other crustaceans as well as on fishes and can sometimes be seen feeding near the surface beneath a flock of feeding seabirds. They weigh about 350 kg at birth, and adults reach 10 tons. Minke whales are known worldwide but are more common in the cooler oceans. They are still abundant in Antarctic waters, numbering about 450 000 in summer. They often swim in schools of 10 to 50 animals. Some populations may be resident in one area all year round.

Sei whales *Balaenoptera borealis* occur worldwide in warm and cool waters, mainly in the open sea beyond the continental shelf. Those in our waters are generally migrating northwards for breeding, or southwards for feeding. They reach a size of about 20 m and 37 tons. They typically move in small schools of three to eight individuals but aggregate in larger groups on the feeding-grounds. They feed on small planktonic animals using their fine-fringed baleen, often skimming along the water surface.

Bryde's whales *Balaenoptera edeni* occur in warm tropical and subtropical waters in the Pacific, Atlantic and Indian Oceans. They feed on small midwater shoaling fishes, such as anchovy, maasbanker and pilchards, as well as on squids, seabirds and sharks. They reach a size of 13 m in males and 13.6 m in females.

The largest whale in South African waters is the **blue whale** *Balaenoptera musculus*, which reaches 33 m in length and a weight of 120 tons (rarely 190 tons), the equivalent weight of 140–150 motorcars. They have 250–400 black baleen plates on each side of the jaw. The blue whale has a heart the size of a Volkswagen beetle, and its tongue weighs

4 tons! The shower of water vapour that they blow from their blow holes is 8–11 m high and can be seen from a distance of 14 km. Their name is derived from the patches of blue markings on their backs. They can swim at speeds of 18–20 km/h for up to 12 hours at a time and sometimes occur in groups of 40–50 animals. They were once thought to be the largest animals that have ever lived but recent finds of giant reptile fossils suggest that there were larger dinosaurs on land in bygone eras. They are certainly the largest-ever mammals.

Blue whales were hunted close to extinction this century and their mortality rates were so high that they may never recover. Their original population in the southern hemisphere numbered about 200 000 but only about 1% is left. They are now patchily distributed worldwide, mainly in cold waters and open seas, migrating southwards in summer to feed on krill. Three to four tons of krill a day are consumed and the energy gained is stored in the blubber.

The second-largest whale in South African waters is the **fin whale** *Balaenoptera physalus,* which reaches 22–24 m in length and 110–140 tons in weight. It has a single ridge on the snout, and the lower jaw and chin are white on the right and black on the left. The dorsal fin is small and sharply pointed, and is directed backwards. In the past they were caught off Durban and Saldanha during their breeding migrations to the north. Fin whales are whales of the high seas, not often encountered inshore. They feed on krill and incidentally caught fishes. They are the fastest and most active of the baleen whales and were seldom caught by early whalers. Even modern whalers have difficulty catching them as they reach speeds of over 30 km/h. Fin whales were the main species caught after the Second World War; their population was reduced from about 400 000 to less than 8 400. They live to an age of at least 40 years.

Two species of **pilot whales** occur in southern Africa. They reach a length of about 6 m and feed on fishes and squid. They may occur in large groups; a pod of 2 800 individuals was seen off Saldanha in 1964.

Killer whales or orcas, *Orcinus orca*, are in fact the largest of the dolphins, and are occasionally seen off the South African coast. They are probably the most widespread of all cetaceans, and are common in the Antarctic and sub-Antarctic and are often seen off Marion Island in summer. They have even been recorded swimming up rivers in England, feeding on salmon! Killer whales are distinguished by their high dorsal fin (2–2.5 m high) which sticks straight up in adult males and curves backwards in young males and females, and by their massive, paddle-shaped flippers. They have striking coloration with the back shiny black and the belly bright white. There is a distinctive white patch behind the eye.

Killer whales reach a size of 9 metres and 8 tons and have large teeth. They are fast-swimming and carnivorous and feed on large prey such as squids, fishes, penguins, turtles, seals, sea lions, elephant seals, dolphins and even the young of large whales. They typically occur in herds of

5–50 animals and are expert social hunters that chase their prey in packs. When hunting dolphins, a group of killer whales may surround them in a circle; one whale then rushes in to catch its prey. They jointly attack large whales and seem to feed selectively on the tongues and blubber. Killer whales are able to strand themselves deliberately in order to catch elephant seals or sea lions, and may even rock ice floes to tip their prey into the water! Captain Scott's expedition to the Antarctic reported that killer whales attempted to catch men walking on the ice floes. Killer whales are not known to have attacked humans under water, although they are inquisitive, but they are dangerous animals and should be respected. They have been seen to look after injured companions.

A related species, the **false killer whale** *Pseudorca crassidens*, is smaller, more slender, with a shorter dorsal fin, no beak, and uniform black coloration. Mass strandings of false killer whales have been recorded off the South African coast. They reach a length of 5.8 m in males and 5 m in females, and can swim at speeds of 22 km/h. The **pygmy killer whale** *Feresa attenuata* was first recorded in the southern hemisphere when five stranded in the lagoon at Luderitz in Namibia. They reach 2.6 m in males and 2.45 m in females, and are known to attack dolphins. Both species feed on squids and fishes and are often found in the company of dolphins. One specimen of a **melon-headed whale** *Peponocephala electra* stranded at Hout Bay in the Cape peninsula in 1976 and was found to have eaten squids and fishes. They are now known to be social animals that live in schools of 100–500 individuals in the open sea.

The **sperm whale** or cachalot, *Physeter macrocephalus*, is the largest of the toothed whales, reaching a weight of 60 tons (usually 20–50 tons) and a length of 15–18 m in males and 11–12 m in females. Females grow to an age of 50–55 years while males reach 40–45 years. They have huge, square heads (one-third the body length), small flippers, a Y-shaped lower jaw, a low hump in place of a fin on the back, a single slit-like blow hole and a dark body with wrinkled skin. They are capable of diving to great depths (over 1 100m) and can hold their breath for up to 90 minutes.

Sperm whales are worldwide in distribution but are rarely seen near the coast, preferring water deeper than 300 m. They are known to swim very long distances. One male tagged in 1961 in the North Atlantic Ocean was killed by whalers operating from the land station at Saldanha Bay in 1966, a direct distance of 7 400 km. The females are known to form large breeding schools of dozens or hundreds of individuals and usually inhabit warmer waters than the males. One shoal of females spotted off Durban in 1972 included over 700 individuals.

Sperm whales have teeth and feed on midwater squid and fishes, including sharks. Their daily food consumption has been estimated at 300 kg for males and 150 kg for females. A giant squid measuring 4.96 m and 184 kg was found in the stomach of a specimen caught in the Azores. Epic battles between sperm whales and giant squid have

Sperm whale in the Southern Ocean. (Photo: Ken Findlay)

been described by early sailors. Early estimates of the size of the squid prey (in excess of 15 m) were made by measuring the width of the squid's sucker marks on the whale's skin. These estimates may be inaccurate as it has been found that the sucker marks grow as the whale increases in size.

When angry, sperm whales can become dangerous and there are many authenticated accounts of their ramming ships with their heads, striking them with their tail flukes or attempting to bite them with their teeth. Many lives were lost among the early whalers when their rowing-boats were capsized by irate sperm whales.

Sperm whales communicate by means of clicks that can be heard up to 10 kilometres away underwater. An oil contained in the head, called spermaceti, may be used by the whale to maintain balance or as a means of focusing sounds. Spermaceti was originally thought to be whale sperm and is prized as a high-quality industrial lubricant. It is one of the only whale products not produced synthetically to high standards and is sought after by space agencies and used as a lubricant in space craft.

A **pygmy** and a **dwarf sperm whale** also occur in southern African waters. They reach 3.5 metres in length and feed on squid, prawns, crabs and fishes.

The **southern bottlenose whale** *Hyperoodon planifrons* has a bulbous forehead, dolphin-like beak and bluish-black to yellowish coloration. It reaches a weight of 6-8 tons and feeds on fish, squid and other invertebrates.

Beaked whales, of which there are 8 species in southern

Africa, are very poorly studied. Many species are only known from South Africa from the carcasses or skulls of stranded animals. They range in length from 4–12 metres and rarely come close inshore.

Behaviour of whales

Whales display several common behaviour patterns that can easily be seen from the shore; these include breaching, lob-tailing, spyhopping, tail-sailing and playing with kelp. The smaller whales and dolphins may also be subject to stranding.

When a whale breaches it rises out of the water head first and then crashes down to one side with a massive splash. *Breaching* is a multipurpose behaviour pattern that allows whales to communicate with one another but also helps with the moulting process (shedding the skin) and with the removal of parasites. When breaching, the whale raises its head well above the surface and then turns or falls backwards onto the water surface with the back strongly arched. After a whale has breached, sea gulls can often be seen picking up lice and pieces of skin from the water surface. Southern right whales breach repetitively, sometimes as often as ten to fifteen times in succession. Breaching is thought by some scientists to be a form of epidictic behaviour, i.e. a way of informing other whales about how many individuals there are in a given area, which may influence breeding rates. Whale calves often breach and seem to do it as an expression of youthful exuberance.

Southern right whale breaching off the South African south coast (Photo: Ken Findlay)

Breaching (top); lobtailing (centre); sailing and spyhopping (below)

	Southern right whale	Humpback whale	Bryde's whale
blow			
tail			
flipper			
head			
back			

Lobtailing or tail-slapping is a form of communication which is often used between mothers and their calves. The whale lies parallel to the water surface and smashes its tail fluke on the water to make a loud smacking sound. Lobtailing may be repeated several times in a row.

Spyhopping involves the whale sticking its head out of the water and holding this position with powerful thrusts of the tail fluke. Whales seem to be naturally curious and have good eyesight above water. Spyhopping may therefore simply be a means of observing what is going on above the water surface.

When it is *tail-sailing* the whale stands on its head in the water with its tail sticking above the water surface. This is thought by some whale observers to be a way in which the whale moves through the water using its tail as a sail, but this is an unlikely explanation for a 30-ton animal that is a very capable swimmer. It may, rather, be a form of play, as it will often swim back to the starting point and do it again. An alternative explanation is that tail-sailing is a means of temperature control whereby the whale loses heat through the numerous blood vessels that permeate the skin of the tail, which is not covered with blubber as is the rest of the body. The tail flukes are also thrown high into the air prior to a deep dive, in an action known as *fluking*. This helps them to achieve a steeper angle for the dive.

Playing with kelp is often observed off the west coast, where the whales actively manipulate pieces of floating kelp so that the fronds rub over their backs and heads, possibly to remove parasites and loose pieces of skin. Whales can also be seen rubbing their backs and heads against the upright fronds of living kelp.

Stranding occurs when whales beach themselves on land. There are many explanations for stranding, including incorrect navigation, loss of orientation due to parasites or diseases, and interference by ships. Mass strandings of small whales and dolphins are often caused by interferences with the navigation of the animal. Cetaceans are known to use the Earth's geomagnetic field for navigation and there is evidence that strandings most often occur in areas where geomagnetic fields have been disturbed. The animals therefore become disoriented and end up on the beach. Why they do not pick up other clues, such as increased wave action or reduced water depth, and react to these in time is not known. As noted above, killer whales can deliberately strand themselves to catch sea lions.

Other less commonly observed behaviours include the fluke swirl (raising one or both tail flukes above the water without slapping the water), tail-up dive, rolling, flipper wave, arching the back, and flipper-slapping.

The *breeding behaviour* of southern right whales is relatively well known as it occurs close to shore. Southern right whales first appear off the South African coast in June and increase in abundance in July with maximum abundance in August, September and October. There are fewer animals in coastal waters in November and December and the last whales usually leave our shores in January. The

41

Flipper wave by a southern right whale. (Photo: Ken Findlay)

number of individual whales seen during the off season, i.e. February to March, is increasing due to the general increase in size of the whale population.

The right whales that are seen close inshore are almost always females with or without calves. In the past, the commercial catch of whales off the South African coast consisted almost entirely of mothers and their calves that were caught close inshore. Groups of large adults, possibly males, may sometimes be seen breaching and lobtailing inshore, usually in bays that are not being used by nursing mothers. These may be groups of males that are competing with one another for access to the females for mating.

When mating, southern right whales lie belly to belly. A number of males attempt to mate with a single female. She may take evasive action by fleeing into shallow water or by rolling onto her back or side. Mating is brief and each of the males may successfully mate with the same female. Sperm selection then takes place in that the sperm race one another to reach the egg first. The gestation period is about 12 months. With rare exceptions whales give birth to one young at a time; pregnant females have been found carrying several foetuses (as many as seven) but it seems that only one is normally born alive.

The calves are born over a four-month period from June to September, with a peak in August off South Africa. The calf is born underwater, near the surface, and normally comes out tail first. The newborn calf sometimes needs to be helped to the surface for its first breath by the mother or an assistant as it is a little awkward initially. Very few births have been seen in the wild.

During calving the females select sheltered bays with gently sloping, sandy bottoms, conditions that are typically found off an estuary. The whales remain in the bay for 3 or 4 months feeding their calf until it is large enough to begin the long migration southwards. Females may return to the same bay to nurse their next calf but may also visit other bays. While they are nursing their young the mothers do not feed; in fact, feeding activity by any large baleen whale is rarely seen off the South African coast.

Southern right whales are playful and inquisitive animals. Though they are slow, lumbering swimmers, they are surprisingly acrobatic. They sometimes swim near the water surface with their mouths agape and the baleen visible. They often bump, push and toss floating objects in the water. Often they take turns to rise to the surface so that only one animal in a group may be visible at a time. Adults sometimes make bellowing sounds and moans during the breeding season. They are rarely washed up on beaches.

Male humpback whales compete for access to females by singing and fighting. In contrast, southern right whale males mob the female, and all the males mate with her. Competition is therefore at the sperm level so that the male that produces the most sperm will have the greatest chance of siring the calf. As far as we know, male southern right whales play no role in raising the calf.

The gestation period of sperm whales is 15-16 months

and the calves are 4 m long at birth. The calves are suckled for one to two years by young mothers, and for three or more years by older mothers. Although solid food is taken by the calf after about one year, some calves have been found with traces of milk in their stomachs at 13 years of age! Female sperm whales are able to start breeding at a length of 8.5 m and an age of 9 years whereas males usually become reproductively active at about 12.5 m and 20 years.

Sperm whales are known to look after their young in groups and to defend them against the attacks of killer whales. The males engage in fearsome fights that involve wrestling, locking their jaws and biting out large chunks of blubber. They do not appear to bite the squid that they eat and it has been suggested that the teeth are only used for fighting among males.

Blue whales start breeding at a size of 23.5 m in females at an age of five years. The gestation period is about 11 months and the young are fed for six to seven months. The young are born tail first, an adaptation to aquatic life. This delays the need to breathe air until the calf is free and can be assisted to the surface by its mother. There is some evidence that blue whales are calving more frequently now than before as a response to increased food availability resulting from the depletion of whale stocks. The calves weigh about 2.5 tons at birth with a length of 7 m. When the calf is weaned seven months later it weighs 23 tons!

In minke whales breeding starts at an age of 7.5 m in

males and 8 m in females. The calving interval is 14 months and the calf is about 2.7 m long when born. They feed from the mother for at least six months. The gestation period of sei whales is about 12 months and the calves are born at a length of 4.5 m and weaned at 8 m. The calving interval is two years.

Our knowledge of the *feeding behaviour* of southern right whales in summer and autumn is relatively poor. We know that the great baleen whales swim through the water, often near the surface, with their cavernous mouths open. They filter out the krill and other small crustaceans that float in the water with their baleen plates. Some species venture as far southwards as the ice edge of the Antarctic continent but most forage in the open waters of the Southern Ocean.

Some whales live and feed in social groups, while others have a more solitary existence. Feeding and breeding behaviours are strongly linked to social organisation and the way in which the whale interprets its environment. Humpback whales are the only baleen whales that feed co-operatively. As we have described, groups of these whales form remarkable bubble nets by releasing curtains of bubbles into the water and entrapping fish and squid. The fish are reluctant to swim through the bubbles and are eaten by the whales before they can escape. Many dolphin species feed co-operatively and some have even taken to fishing co-operatively with humans. Killer whales are exceptionally well-organised pack hunters that are able to subdue large or elusive prey that they would not otherwise be able to catch as individuals, such as penguins and seals.

Some whales and dolphins are capable of diving to great depths. Sperm whales dive to over 1 100 m, fin whales to 500 m, and killer whales and bottlenosed dolphins to at least 300 m. Deep diving is usually linked to feeding behaviour. As baleen whales feed on prey near the surface, they are generally shallower divers, rarely diving deeper than a few hundred metres.

Early use of whales

Although whales have not had as direct an impact on the lives of South Africans as they have had on the peoples of, for instance, New Zealand, Greenland or Canada, they have been an important source of food and other products for several thousand years. The early indigenous people at the southern tip of Africa, the Khoi-San, made extensive use of the meat, oil and blubber of stranded whales. Some estimates reveal that as much as 10% of the diet of coastal Khoi-San people may have been derived from whale products. The blubber was used to produce oil that was either drunk directly or used for frying fish or red meat. As it was not possible to use all the meat and oil from a stranded whale that may have weighed 30 or 40 tons, various ways of preserving the meat were devised. The meat and blubber were stored for up to 10 days by burial in wet sand. The meat was also dried in the sun for use later or for transport inland. The Khoi-San also used the rib bones and mandibles of stranded whales to make huts, and may have used the baleen to roof their huts. The giant vertebrae were used as seats. This sustainable use of whale products lasted for over 1 800 years until the wholesale massacre of whales during the whaling era.

Today the indigenous people of several countries where whales are important, such as New Zealand, Canada and Greenland, are the prime movers in the development of a whale-watching industry. For instance, in New Zealand one of the main boat-based whale-watching operations is run by Maoris.

History of whaling

Whales have been hunted by man ever since we set out to sea in boats. The Inuit or Eskimos were one of the first peoples to hunt whales from boats. They used skin-covered whale boats or umiaks and hand-thrown harpoons. Today the International Whaling Commission allows a subsistence catch of whales to peoples who have traditionally hunted them.

European whaling was first practised by the Basques of northern Spain, who were catching right whales in the Bay of Biscay in the twelfth century. By the 1600s the French, English, Dutch, Danes, Norwegians, Germans and Portuguese were all whaling off the coast of Europe – using hand-thrown harpoons from open boats. Soon after Jan van Riebeeck landed in South Africa to start a refreshment station at the Cape of Good Hope, the Dutch government decided to exploit the whales that were commonly observed in Table Bay. They sent out whaling boats from Holland but subsequently abandoned the venture as they found the whales to be too small and to yield too little oil.

By the early 1700s the whaling industry had reached the east coast of America and by the late 1700s whaling vessels were hunting throughout the southern hemisphere. By 1785 British, French and American fleets were hunting southern right whales off the southern African coast, and in 1792 the colonists in South Africa were given permission to exploit the local whale stocks. In 1806, when the British seized the Cape, whaling developed rapidly in Table Bay and False Bay. In 1820 the whaling station operated from Robben Island was closed when the Xhosa chief Makhanda and 30 other prisoners escaped from the island in the boats of a local whaler (John Murray). Makhanda was drowned near the shore but some of the other prisoners escaped onto the mainland, most being recaptured.

Between 1785 and 1805 some 12 000 southern right whales were taken from the southern African coastline. The unexploited population of over 20 000 southern right whales producing between 1 000 and 2 000 calves a year was suddenly decimated and for about 150 years a remnant population was all that survived off the South African coast. In 1817 a record catch of 76 whales was made off the South African coast and in 1822 whaling was rivalled only by wine-making and agriculture as the most lucrative occupation in the Cape of Good Hope.

By the 1840s the whale catch had dropped to about one-fifth of the population 30 years before and the industry had basically collapsed by the year 1900. The foreign fleets moved on to exploit other whale stocks but a small-scale local effort continued into the twentieth century. By the time the first measures were introduced to protect whales in 1935 their numbers had dwindled to less than 1% of the unexploited population sizes, and only 30–60 individuals were found off the South African coast.

Modern whaling using cannon-fired harpoons from a motorised catcher started in the southern hemisphere (South Georgia, Antarctica) in 1904 and in South Africa (in Durban) in 1908. Humpback whales were initially targeted. Between 1908 and 1917 an estimated 25 000 humpbacks were taken in southern African waters. Whaling in South Africa continued until 1975.

The introduction of open-water factory ships in the late 1920s opened the Antarctic region to whaling. Humpback catches were followed by blue, then fin and sei whale catches. By the 1960s the blue whale and the humpback whale had been reduced to about 6 and 7% respectively of their original population sizes. One of the most dramatic collapses of a whale stock occurred in recent times when the abundance of sei whales fell by about 80% between 1965 and 1967 at both the Durban and Donkergat whaling stations. In the 1970s only the small minke whale survived in the Antarctic in reasonable numbers. Throughout the world the history of whaling has been characterised by the repeated overexploitation of regional and global whale stocks.

Today many of the world's whale populations have been reduced to less than 10% of their original numbers although some, but not all, are making a strong recovery. In South Africa, and on their other breeding-grounds, the southern right whale population is increasing at 7–8% per year. In the southern hemisphere, humpback whale populations are increasing at 8–10% per year, one of the strongest recoveries anywhere.

At the time that these estimates were originally made, conventional wisdom suggested that this intrinsic rate of increase was too high and could not be sustained. However, the whales confounded the critics and have sustained these exceptionally high rates of recovery. Recent censuses by Dr Peter Best have revealed that as many as 139 cow–calf pairs occur off the South African coast compared to just 20 pairs 25 years ago. The population of southern right whales is nevertheless still at about 10% of its pristine level, but it is probably out of danger.

Many place names along the southern African coast bear testimony to the importance of whales and whaling in bygone ages, such as Walvis Bay, Grainger Bay, Murray's Bay and Miller's Point, the latter three named after well-known whalers.

A similar pattern of whale exploitation occurred in Australia. Shore-based whaling started there in 1805, mainly from French, British and American vessels. Between 1827 and 1899 over 26 000 southern right whales were caught, with three-quarters of the catch being made in the 1830s and 1840s. One American vessel was reported to have killed 33 whales in three months! Predictably, the whale stocks collapsed and by the early 1900s whales were hardly ever sighted off Australia. Their stocks recovered slowly and by the 1960s they were again being sighted regularly. Today whales off Australia are strictly protected and they are recovering at a rate of about 7% per annum.

In the northern hemisphere the situation is not as optimistic. The northern right whale is probably closer to extinction than any other large whale and may never recover; it may already be doomed to extinction in the North Atlantic Ocean, where it was once abundant. Some southern hemisphere whale species, such as the blue whale, are also recovering slowly.

The cessation of whaling alone may not result in the full recovery of whale populations to pre-whaling levels as many other factors, such as heavy ship traffic, chemical and noise pollution underwater, competition for food with commercial fishing enterprises and global environmental impacts on their food resources, may also threaten their survival. The survival of the remaining whale stocks will depend both on the changed attitude that most people now have towards them, and on an increased understanding of their living requirements that is developed through further research on whales and their habitats.

Whales were not only harvested for their meat and oil

but also for their baleen or 'whale bone'. Before the invention of plastics, baleen was in demand for a multiple of purposes in everyday life, from brushes, combs, umbrella ribs to women's corsets. Whale oil was used as a lubricant and lamp fuel as well as to make soap, margarine, ice cream, candles and to soften leather. Today alternatives have been found for all whale products except spermaceti, although whale meat is still regarded as a gourmet dish in Japan.

Ambergris, which was extensively used in making perfumes, is a substance produced in the rectum of the sperm whale, apparently as a result of the irritation caused by squid beaks. It is a sticky, blackish-brown substance when fresh, with a strong smell. Lumps of ambergris are occasionally washed up on the shore.

Whales, man and whale watching

The bond between people and whales can be traced back to pre-biblical times, when dolphins were considered to be sacred animals and whales were feared as destructive monsters.

These beliefs collapsed during the whaling era when whales were ruthlessly exploited. Recently we have come to respect whales as some of the most magnificent creatures that have ever evolved, and they have become a symbol of the 'green' movement.

As far back as 1500 BC Greek and Roman artists depicted dolphins in art and on coins. Authors and poets of the

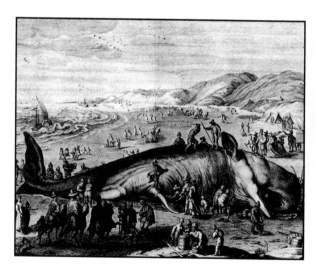

Sperm whale stranded on a Dutch beach in 1601. The local people thought it was an evil omen.

Mediterranean region regarded cetaceans as sacred animals. In Greek mythology creation was thought to have been linked to dolphins. Many of the Greek and Roman stories about dolphins refer to the friendship between dolphins and children and to their reputation for saving shipwrecked sailors. Dolphins also symbolised safety and virtue.

During Biblical and medieval times whales were largely feared as sea monsters and were often depicted devouring ships. During the whaling era our outlook on whales changed to exploitation and greed. The last twenty years has seen modern Man's attitude to whales change to one of protection and preservation. Non-consumptive uses of whales, such as whale watching, have become very popular worldwide.

Whale watching is the fastest-growing sector of the eco-tourism industry in the world and is growing at a rate of 49% according to Dr Ken Findlay, who has conducted research in this field.

Whale watching includes land-, boat- and aerial-based whale watching as well as dolphin watching, swimming with dolphins and dolphin-feeding activities. About 72% of the world's whale watching is boat-based and about 27% land-based. Whale watching originated in California in 1955. By 1994, 65 different nations were offering whale or dolphin watching as a tourism activity. The world's whale-watching industry was worth over US $504 million in 1994 when an estimated 5.4 million people participated.

There are 37 species of whales and dolphins off the coast

of southern Africa but not all of these species are suited to whale watching. The most commonly sighted species is the southern right whale, as 90% of their winter and spring migrants to South Africa approach to within one kilometre of the shore, and some within 40 metres. The other species that can be seen from our coast include the humpback and Bryde's whales and Heaviside's, dusky, common, bottlenosed and humpback dolphins.

While initially most whale watchers were content to observe whales from the shore, inevitably some wanted to be closer and to watch them from boats, which brought them into potential conflict with the law. Boat-based whale watching is commonly practised in many countries around the world, and in some countries diving with whales and dolphins is also permitted. A popular method of boat-based whale watching is from kayaks, which allow one to approach the whales with the minimum of disturbance. It has been found, however, that a completely silent approach may alarm the whale so some paddle-slapping or other gentle reminder of your presence is recommended. Many people have found that kayaking with a whale is a life-changing experience.

There are two schools of thought on whether whale watching should be allowed from boats or aircraft in South Africa. Some environmentalists feel that uncontrolled boat-based whale watching may come into conflict with shore-based whale watching, which is one of the fastest growing tourist attractions in South Africa. They object to the disturbance caused by the boats to the whales as well as to shore-based watchers. It is further argued that persistent, noisy boats may cause whales to leave their inshore breeding and calving grounds for less suitable, offshore environments where they would be less visible to shore-based watchers. They urge a precautionary approach to whale watching to avoid a free-for-all situation that could chase the whales away as well as detrimentally affect their strong recovery to their original population size.

The risks posed by boat-based whale watching need to be weighed against the potential economic benefits. Because of the inclement weather and rough seas off the southern Cape coast from June to November, there may be many days (perhaps 40%) when boats cannot go out to sea, which may make the activity only marginally economical.

Boat-based whale watching is legal and economical in many countries, such as New Zealand and the USA, but it is strictly controlled. In the USA, large, 33 m boats are used, whereas 16 m boats accommodating 60 people are preferred in New Zealand. It is very unlikely that large boats will be allowed for whale watching in South Africa. A large-boat operator who tried to launch a whale-watching business off a south coast resort in South Africa was hounded out of town by the locals because of their strong sense of ownership of the whales.

Whale watching from fixed-wing aircraft and helicopters is also practised in the western Cape. One operator uses a seaplane and lands on the sea in the vicinity of whales and dolphins. A hydrophone is lowered into the water and cetacean songs are played to attract whales and dolphins in the vicinity of the seaplane. Research in New Zealand has revealed that an aircraft's noise causes little disturbance to whales, whereas the shadow passing overhead does cause a reaction. The noise from the aircraft does not seem to disturb the whale as long as the aircraft stays outside a 13-degree cone above the whale.

Research in South Africa by Ken Findlay has revealed that carefully executed boat-based whale watching has virtually no impact on the behaviour of nearby whales. The most disturbance under experimental situations using one small motorboat was caused when the boat approached the whale from the front. Research in New Zealand and the USA has revealed that outboard motors cause more disturbance to whales than inboard motors as the former create a great deal more noise underwater and often cavitate (cause air bubbles). New four-stroke outboard motors are far quieter and may be more suited to boat-based whale watching, when it is allowed in South Africa.

The National Association of Professional Whale Guides aims to deliver a positive input into whale tourism and to promote boat-based whale watching in future. They argue that, of all the funds generated by whale watching worldwide, boat-based watching contributes more than 75% of the income. They plan to educate boat skippers and the general public about the potential impacts of boat-based watching, to evaluate and control the impacts and to set standards for whale watching and whale conservation. They point out that the demand for whale watching by local and foreign tourists justifies a detailed investigation of the ways in which boat-based watching can take place without disturbing the whales.

Whale legislation

The Sea Fisheries authorities have decided boat-based whale watching will be allowed in South Africa on a limited basis. In order to control the degree of disturbance caused by boats and other traffic on whales, a regulation prohibiting (and defining) harassment of whales was adopted in 1980 as part of the Sea Fisheries Act, 1973. As amended in 1984, and now incorporated under the Sea Fisheries Act. 1988, this regulation (no. 30) now reads:

- '(1) Except under the authority of a permit issued by the Director-General, no person shall catch, kill, disturb or harass any whale at any time;
- (2) For the purposes of subparagraph (1), "disturb or harass" shall also include –
- (a) the shooting of any whale;
- (b) approaching closer than 300 metres to any whale, by means of a vessel, aircraft or other device;
- (c) that, in the event of a whale surfacing closer than 300 metres from a vessel, the person in charge of such vessel fails to proceed immediately to a distance of at

least 300 metres from the whale;
- but shall not include bona fide efforts by any person to render aid to a stranded or beached whale.'

The enforcement of these regulations, which are currently under review, is the responsibility of inspection officials of the provincial conservation authorities or parks boards. So far (May 1998) sixteen boat-based whale watching permits have been issued in South Africa, although this activity has been carried out illegally in various bays since 1990. It is likely that further experimental boat-based whale watching will be carried out before further permits are issued, but the illegal activities will first need to be controlled.

There is little firm evidence from research in several countries to suggest that controlled boat-based whale watching has negative impacts on whale or dolphin populations, but it is a difficult subject on which to conduct research. If the whales or dolphins are disturbed, chased or fed over a long period, there may well be unwanted and subtle impacts. For instance, the feeding of wild dolphins has been shown to have negative impacts on calf and juvenile survival in New Zealand, as the mothers abandon their calves in order to feed inshore and consequently do not teach the calves how to hunt.

Experience gained elsewhere will be taken into account in the promulgation of new whale-watching legislation in South Africa. When boat-based whale watching is allowed, it is likely to be confined to coastal areas which do not have suitable shore-based watching sites. The use of inboard-powered boats with emission controls is likely to be favoured over outboard-powered boats. The use of jetskis for whale watching will almost certainly not be allowed. Only one boat at a time is likely to be allowed to approach within 300 metres of a whale.

In some places, such as Hawaii, where whale-watching regulations are very strictly enforced, boat skippers use rangefinders to measure the distance between them and the whales so as to ensure that they do not approach too closely. In order to prevent whales from feeling trapped or being disturbed, boats are only allowed to approach a whale from behind and slightly to one side; head-on or tail-on approaches are not allowed. Other codes of conduct include: always move slowly, do not separate groups of whales, avoid sudden changes of speed or direction, do not stay longer than 15 minutes, and, when leaving, move off at a 'no wake' speed for the first few hundred metres.

Whale-watching tips

If you observe a few commonsense precautions, you will be able to watch whales without disturbing them, and will therefore be able to witness their natural behaviour. As whales are sensitive to disturbance, try to make minimum noise and to encourage others also to be quiet; never throw objects into the water, thereby causing the whales to move away. While watching whales, stay on demarcated paths and be careful that you do not trample coastal vegetation. Always respect the rights of private land-owners and keep off private land. When you are standing on a rocky shore be careful of slippery rocks and beware of freak waves that may wash you out to sea.

The MTN Cape Whale Route, which was established in February 1996, is the first tourism development project sponsored by a commercial company in South Africa. The project aims to market whale watching along the coasts of the northern and western Cape and to promote education, training and conservation programmes on whales. Whales, along with the lion, elephant, buffalo, rhinoceros and giraffe, now comprise the 'big six' of African game watching. Whale watching provides a tremendous boost to the eco-tourism industry and promotes sustainable coastal development. The MTN Cape Whale Route has recently extended its ecotourism and environmental education initiatives to include the flowers of Namaqualand, the black oystercatcher (one of southern Africa's rarest coastal birds), and the continental populations of African penguins, such as those at Boulders and Betty's Bay.

The MTN Cape Whale Route also strongly supports the whale and other environmental education programmes of the Two Oceans Environmental Education Trust at the Two Oceans Aquarium in Cape Town.

Whale-watching sites

South Africa has some of the world's best land-based whale-watching sites. These sites rely on the nearshore breeding migrations of the southern right whale along the western and eastern Cape coasts in winter, spring and early summer. The whales come very close inshore, typically just outside the last line of breakers from the beach, and their behaviour is clearly visible.

Most southern right whales are seen off our coast in September, followed by August, October, November, July, December and June respectively. The main southern right whale-watching area stretches from Lambert's Bay on the west coast to Algoa Bay in the east, although they are occasionally seen to the north and east of these sites. Humpback whales are seen off the South African west coast northwards into Namibia and along the east coast through the eastern Cape and KwaZulu-Natal into Mozambique.

Whales were sufficiently abundant in Table Bay and False Bay in the late 1800s and early 1900s to support whaling stations there. These areas do not compare well today with other sites farther east, possibly due to disturbance by ships and other factors. Nevertheless excellent views of whales can sometimes be made from Yzerfontein, Melkbosstrand and Robben Island to the north of Table Bay, and from Llandudno, Hout Bay, Chapman's Peak Drive, Scarborough and Assegaaibosch on the west coast of the Cape Peninsula. The view over Chapman's Bay and Long

Beach from the southern end of Chapman's Peak Drive is particularly spectacular. Within False Bay there is sometimes excellent whale watching from the restaurant at Cape Point looking northwards into the Bay as well as from sites around the coast of False Bay, such as Smitswinkelbaai, Miller's Point, Fish Hoek, St James, Gordon's Bay and Cape Hangklip. A trip along Boyes Drive, situated high above Muizenberg, will give you a good idea of where the whales are on the west side of False Bay, but you will need binoculars from there.

Whales occur more frequently along the west coast to the north of Cape Town than in the Cape Peninsula area. Good sites are found at Melkbosstrand, Bok Point, Yzerfontein and off Saldanha Bay, especially at Plankiesbaai, just to the north of Vondeling Island. As Plankiesbaai is within the West Coast National Park, you will have to obtain permission to enter the area and you should check beforehand about accessibility. Farther north whales can be seen in the vicinity of St Helena Bay at Cape Columbine, the Rocher Pan Nature Reserve, Elands Bay, Stompneuspunt and in Paternoster Bay.

The best whale-watching sites in South Africa are found between Cape Hangklip and Witsand. Whales can sometimes be sighted in Sandown Bay and Kleinmond to the east of Cape Hangklip, but the self-proclaimed whale-watching capital of South Africa is Hermanus. Find the promontory overlooking the Old Harbour (where there is an interesting museum with displays on whales), and follow the delightful clifftop walks to the east and west. Groups of people usually gather on each headland to watch the whales within a few hundred metres of the shore. Over 10 000 whale watchers descend on Hermanus each month in the high season and they may spend up to R5.4 million in one week, according to research done by Ken Findlay. If you don't see whales there, there are probably none to be seen! To the east of Hermanus whales can also be sighted from Gansbaai and Die Kelders.

The best shore-based whale watching in the world is probably found in De Hoop Nature Reserve, especially at Koppie Alleen and Klipkoppie, and eastwards towards Witsand at the Breede River mouth. Over 70% of the cow-calf pairs of southern right whales recorded in South Africa occur in this area; 30 pairs of mothers and calves can sometimes be observed at the same time! This is a beautiful, pristine section of coast and, though difficult to reach, the journey is well worthwhile. De Hoop Nature Reserve is reached via Bredasdorp, whereas Witsand is accessed via Swellendam. De Hoop Nature Reserve has the added attraction of rich indigenous vegetation as well as bontebok, tortoises, eland, mountain zebra and a variety of birds, including ostriches. The manmade wetland on the western edge of the reserve has a spectacular diversity of waterbirds, including the most southerly populations of flamingos and pelicans in Africa. The tidal pools at Koppie Alleen are bursting with life and the beaches are a paradise for shell collectors. De Hoop is a nature reserve run by Cape Nature

Conservation, and reservations have to be made beforehand for overnight accommodation.

To the east of Witsand the chances of seeing whales close inshore are sharply reduced, although this situation may change as the whale populations increase. The best sites are found in the large half-moon bays that are such a characteristic feature of the south coast, especially in the vicinities of river mouths. The sheltered Mossel Bay is a good spot, as whales sometimes gather between Seal Island and Glentana. The bluff adjacent to the freeway just to the west of Wilderness (known as Dolphin Lookout) is also a good site as it offers a panoramic view of the coast to the east and west. If you catch the coastal train you could even do some whale spotting from a train, as the railway line crosses the river mouth at this point and travels adjacent to the coast.

The next major bay along the coast is Plettenberg Bay, and this is also the next best whale-watching site. Although Robberg peninsula offers spectacular elevated views over the bay, the whales are usually found farther inshore and the best viewing sites are within the town, especially from Beacon Island or Lookout Rocks. Few cow–calf pairs have been recorded in this area in recent censuses but this situation may change in future.

Nature's Valley at the mouth of the Grootrivier is one of South Africa's most scenic coastal resorts and offers occasional but spectacular whale and dolphin watching from the high bluff to the east of the beach (which marks the end of the Otter Trail). An even better site is beyond the west

nd of the beach on a steep bluff overlooking the Soutrivier
mouth. Bottlenosed and humpback dolphins are frequently
seen along this stretch of coast, often within the breaker
line.

Whale research

Much of what we know about whales comes from information collected from whales that were caught by the commercial whaling industry. During this era researchers had
access to a large number of carcasses from which they could
collect data. Today, with the cessation of whaling, whale
research has centred on non-lethal ways of collecting information, such as population censuses using aeroplanes,
photo-identification and genetic studies.

One of the main areas of interest in research on whales
is their rate of recovery from whaling. Population counts of
whales are carried out from aircraft or ships or from land.
Such observations are difficult as the animals spend much
of their time out of sight, and they migrate considerable distances between seasons. The population sizes of many of
the world's smaller whales are unknown. The status of the
larger whales is better known and scientists have been able
to track their recovery with some accuracy.

Individuals of many whale species can be recognised
from their characteristic body features. These features
include the dorsal fin and tail fluke shape, and the patterns
of scarring, coloration and callosities (wartlike skin growths
on the head). Although such individuals are difficult to

recognise by eye in the wild, they can easily be recognised from photographs. Photo-identification has provided information on population size changes, individual growth rates, migration routes and breeding behaviour. For example, the natural markings (callosities and body coloration) on southern right whales have enabled scientists to collect some very valuable information on population size, movement patterns, calving intervals, growth rates and rates of population increase.

The use of these natural tags has allowed us to calculate for instance, the number of mature female whales in South African waters in a particular year (e.g. 289 in 1987) and the distance migrated by a female photographed off Gough Island in the South Atlantic Ocean in 1983 (it was photographed again at De Hoop Nature Reserve in the Western Cape in 1988 and had travelled at least 2 769 km in five years). The calving interval has been established at 3 years for 80% of the whales sampled, with a few calving every 2 years and some at intervals of 4 or 5 years or longer. The age of first calving ranges between 6 and 10 years and the calves grow at a rate of 2.8 cm per day in South African waters. The annual survival rates of adult southern right whales in South Africa have been calculated as 97–98%.

Fixed-wing aircraft surveys of whales in South Africa were initiated in 1969 and helicopter surveys in 1979. The flights are part of a research programme by well-known whale scientist Dr Peter Best of the Mammal Research Institute, who is based at the South African Museum in

Cape Town. They take place once a year in mid-October along the same flight path from False Bay in the west to Woody Cape on the east side of Algoa Bay. This range covers the likely location of over 90% of all cow–calf pairs in south African waters. The aim of the surveys is to obtain an estimate of population abundance as well as to determine calving intervals, adult and calf survival rates and age at first breeding.

In 1997 129 cow–calf pairs were seen and 474 whales were sighted in total. As many as 70 cow-calf pairs were sighted in some bays. The age at first breeding ranged between 6 and 13 years (average about 9 years).

Similar surveys have been carried out on southern right whales along the south coast of Australia using fixed-wing aircraft. The total population size of males and females is estimated to be between 800 and 1 000 animals. The first calves are produced when the mother is about 9 years old.

Genetic research has recently become an important component of whale research. Small skin samples are easily collected from live whales without harming them. Analyses of DNA material from these samples provides important information on the relationship between individuals within groups, of groups within populations and of populations within a species.

Telemetry is a research technique in which a transmitter is attached to the whale and sends signals back to receivers. Both radio and satellite telemetry has been used in whale research. Although originally used just to track whales, transmitters now send back other information such as dive times and depths. Satellite telemetry could provide a particularly useful tool in research on whale migrations but the technique is limited by the difficulty of attaching the transmitters to the whales.

Today dead stranded whales and dolphins are an important source of research data. Researchers at strandings are usually finding out more about the animals themselves rather than the reason for their stranding. For example, teeth (and earplugs in baleen whales) have growth layers in them which can give hints on the age and growth rate of the animal. Stomach contents can reveal information about their diet, and the examination of the reproductive organs tells us about where and when they breed and how many young they produce.

Whale conservation

In 1946 the International Convention for the Regulation of Whaling was established, with South Africa as one of the founding nations. This led to the establishment of the International Whaling Commission (IWC) which aims 'to provide for the conservation, development and optimum utilisation of the whale resources'. For a number of reasons, some of them political, the IWC failed to prevent the over-exploitation of humpback, blue, fin, sei and, to some extent, sperm whale stocks. Each of these species eventually had to be given total protection from commercial whaling.

In 1982, reacting to overwhelming public pressure, the IWC decided to halt temporarily all commercial whaling so as to allow the stocks to recover and to test the impact of the cessation of whaling. Today whale conservation is increasingly based on solid research although information on many species is still very thin.

The favoured destination of southern right whales in South African waters – the shallow inshore reaches of sheltered bays on the southern coast – brings them into direct conflict with humans, who use the same places for recreational and industrial purposes. The increasing number of people using inshore bays, the escalating sophistication of their recreational 'toys' and the increasing number of whales (including calves) in the inshore zone, are creating a potential conflict situation that is likely to worsen in future. This conflict will only be resolved if everyone has a clear understanding of the problems and sensitivities involved.

Commercial activities also have an impact on cetaceans. Increased fishing activity off the South African coast, as well as shark netting, has increased the bycatch of small whales and dolphins, as has been the case worldwide. The increased volume of ship traffic around the Cape of Good Hope increases the risk of damage or death to even the largest whales.

Whales have an important role to play in the natural functioning of the coastal zone of South Africa and of the whole Southern Ocean system. Now that their numbers are increasing again, it is essential that we give them sufficient space off our coast to breed, calve and feed their young. This can be done without sacrificing coastal development or recreational opportunities for people. In fact, the conservation of whales is likely to enhance long-term coastal development and the development of the full touristic and recreational potential of the coast. A win-win situation can be created if the needs of the whales are taken into account.

Besides the threats of boat-based whale watching discussed above, there are other threats to whales in South Africa. Any form of harassment of whales, which have an acute sense of hearing and touch, could detrimentally affect them. Noisy industries near the shore or intensive motorboat activity or races near their breeding and calving grounds may cause disturbance. The release of untreated or partially treated sewerage effluent or chemical pollutants into the sea should be avoided for the benefit of all sea life. The entanglement of whales and dolphins in fishing gear, such as abandoned gill, trawl and seine nets or crayfish traplines, represents a threat to the smaller species and calves.

Few of these problems are caused by premeditated actions and most are accidental. They are therefore best prevented through better public education, as is occurring through the MTN Cape Whale Route, Two Oceans Aquarium, South African Museum, Dolphin Action and Protection Group, Port Elizabeth Museum, Seaworld in Durban and other institutions, rather than through heavy-handed legislation.

The future of whales

Unlike the land, which is permanently divided up by man's activities, the seas still form a continuous environment that can provide a habitat for vast numbers of marine animals, including whales. Despite our concentrated conservation efforts on land over several decades, we are only able to provide full protection to less than 10% of the land area of South Africa. Even these areas are at the receiving end of environmental impacts that originate far away. Many terrestrial habitats between the formal nature reserves are severely degraded and others have been completely transformed by urbanisation and other forms of development.

The seas have not escaped man's interventions, and they are likely to be affected significantly by global environmental impacts, such as ozone depletion, global warming and increased UV radiation. The krill food stocks of the great baleen whales are particularly threatened by global impacts. Nevertheless, the remarkable recovery of some whale populations following the cessation of commercial whaling activities has made us realise that miracles can occur. We can, as co-inhabitants of this planet with millions of other species, live in relative harmony with our fellow travellers.

The recovery of the southern right whales off our coast should be an inspiration to us all. If we all reduce our impact on the natural environment, the cumulative positive effect will be massive. Other species, on land and in the sea, will also be able to recover, but only if we can control our own population increase and live off the interest rather than the capital of the Earth.

We are the most abundant large animal that has ever evolved on the planet, and the most intelligent. We have evolved at a time when the diversity of plants and animals is higher than it has ever been. We are also the first species that could cause most other species to become extinct.

Whales have several similarities to humans. They are intelligent, warm-blooded mammals that originated on land. They have the same body temperature as ours, and they suckle their young. The great whales reach sexual maturity at about the same age as us, and they also live to the biblical three score years and ten.

So let us enjoy the return of the whales and appreciate the significance of their recovery. And let us translate the experience into a changed mindset and a changed behaviour towards the environment. Even though whales live in the sea and we live on land, we are inextricably bound together by the life-supporting systems of the planet. Our survival depends on them and they depend on us. It is a contract that we should honour.

APPENDIX 1:
What to do if you find a stranded whale or dolphin

If you find a stranded whale or dolphin, immediately inform your local aquarium, museum, nature conservation or fisheries office or police station and give exact details of the location, state of the tide and description of the animal. Keep the animal's skin moist and erect a shelter to provide shade. Try to keep the flippers and tail flukes cool and make sure that the blow hole is facing upwards. Keep onlookers at a distance and make as little noise as possible. Do not stand too close to the whale or push or pull on its flippers or flukes. Under no circumstances should you cover the blow hole or apply suntan lotion to its skin.

If a whale biologist can reach the stranding before it washes out to sea or decomposes, he or she could obtain valuable information about its biology and ecology. It is always tempting to attempt to push the stranded cetacean back into the sea but this may be pointless if it is already severely injured or diseased. Optimal use should then be made of the specimen for research so that the remaining members of the species can be better understood and managed. Even badly decomposed carcasses or skeletons are useful to biologists. Let an expert decide whether or not the animal should be returned to the sea.

APPENDIX 2:
List of whale and dolphin species known from South Africa

Order:	Cetacea	**Whales and dolphins**
Suborder:	Odontoceti	**Toothed whales**
Family:	Ziphiidae	**Beaked whales**
	Berardius arnuxii	Arnoux's beaked whale
	Mesoplodon hectori	Hector's beaked whale
	Mesoplodon mirus	True's beaked whale
	Mesoplodon layardii	Layard's beaked whale
	Mesoplodon densirostris	Blainville's beaked whale
	Mesoplodon grayi	Gray's beaked whale
	Ziphius cavirostris	Cuvier's beaked whale
	Hyperoodon planifrons	Southern bottlenose whale
Family:	Physeteridae	**Sperm whales**
Subfamily	Kogiinae	Pygmy and dwarf sperm whales
	Kogia breviceps	Pygmy sperm whale
	Kogia simus	Dwarf sperm whale

Subfamily	Physeterinae	Sperm whales
	Physeter macrocephalus	Sperm whale
Family	Delphinidae	**Dolphins, pilot whales, killer and false killer whales**
	Grampus griseus	Risso's dolphin
	Globicephala macro-rhynchus	Short-finned pilot whale
	Globicephala melaena	Long-finned pilot whale
	Orcinus orca	Killer whale
	Feresa attenuata	Pygmy killer whale
	Pseudorca crassidens	False killer whale
	Steno bredanensis	Rough-toothed dolphin
	Delphinus delphis	Common dolphin
	Stenella longirostris	Spinner dolphin
	Stenella coeruleoalba	Striped dolphin
	Stenella attenuata	Spotted dolphin
	Sousa plumbea	Humpback dolphin
	Tursiops truncatus	Bottlenosed dolphin
	Lissodelphis peronii	Southern right whale dolphin
	Lagenodelphis hosei	Fraser's dolphin
	Peponocephala electra	Melon-headed whale
	Lagenorhynchus obscurus	Dusky dolphin
	Cephalorhynchus heavisidii	Heaviside's dolphin

Suborder:	Mysticeti	**Baleen whales**
Family:	Balaenidae	**Right whales**
	Eubalaena australis	Southern right whale
Family:	Neobalaenidae	**Pygmy right whales**
	Caperea marginata	Pygmy right whale
Family:	Balaenopteridae	**Rorqual whales**
	Megaptera novaeangliae	Humpback whale
	Balaenoptera acuto-rostrata	Minke whale
	Balaenoptera borealis	Sei whale
	Balaenoptera edeni	Bryde's whale
	Balaenoptera musculus	Blue whale
	Balaenoptera physalus	Fin whale

ACKNOWLEDGEMENTS

I am very grateful to Ken Findlay and Peter Best for their expert advice on whales, and to Peter During of MTN for the opportunity to be involved in the educational programmes of the MTN Cape Whale Route.

Grateful acknowledgements are made also to the MTN Cape Whale Route for their financial contribution towards the costs of this book.

SOURCES AND FURTHER READING

Best, P.B. 'The status of right whales (*Eubalaena glacialis*) off South Africa, 1969–1979'. Investigational Report of the Sea Fisheries Research Institute, South Africa 123: 1–44 (1981).

Best, P.B. *Whale Watching in South Africa: The Southern Right Whale* (Cape Town, 1997).

Best, P.B., and Ross, G.J.B. 'Whales and whaling'. In: *Oceans of Life off Southern Africa* (Cape Town, 1989).

Best, P.B., and Ruther, H. 'Aerial photogrammetry of southern right whales, *Eubalaena australis*'. *J. Zool.* (Lond.), 228: 595–614 (1992).

Best, P.B., and Scott, H.A. 'The distribution, seasonality and trends in abundance of southern right whales *Eubalaena australis* off De Hoop Nature Reserve, South Africa'. *S. Afr. J. Mar. Sci.* 13: 175–186 (1993).

Best, P.B., Crawford, R.J.M., and van der Elst, R.P. 'Top

predators in southern Africa's marine ecosystems'. *Trans. Roy. Soc. S. Afr.* 52(1): 177–225 (1997).

Branch, G.M., Griffiths, C.L., Branch, M.L., and Beckley, L.E. *Two Oceans: A Guide to the Marine Life of Southern Africa* (Cape Town, 1994).

Cawardine, M. *Whales, Dolphins and Porpoises.* (London, 1995).

Papastavrou, V. *Whale* (London, 1993).

Skinner, J.D., and Smithers, R.H.N. *The Mammals of the Southern African Subregion* (Pretoria, 1990).

Waller, G. *Sealife: A Complete Guide to the Marine Environment* (Halfway House, 1996).